Joel M. Lerner's

101 Townhouse Garden Designs*

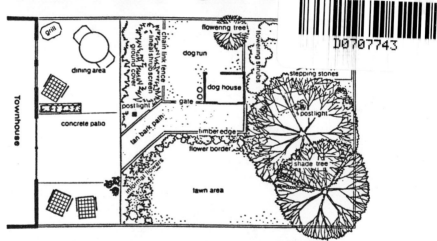

*To Fit Your Personality

HPBooks

Published by HPBooks
A Division of HPBooks, Inc.
P.O. Box 5367
Tucson, AZ 85703
602-888-2150

Publisher: Rick Bailey
Executive Editor: Randy Summerlin

©1985 by Joel M. Lerner
Printed in U.S.A.
1st printing, Revised Edition
Originally published by SANJO Press, Beltsville, Maryland

Library of Congress Cataloguing in Publication Data

Lerner, Joel M. 1947-
   Joel M. Lerner's 101 townhouse garden designs*.
   *Bottom of t.p.: To fit your personality.
   1. Gardens—Designs and plans. I. Title.
II. Title: 101 townhouse garden designs. III. Title:
One hundred one townhouse garden designs. IV. Title:
One hundred and one townhouse garden designs. V. Title:
Townhouse garden designs.
SB473.L46 1987   712'.6   86-45962   ISBN 0-89586-545-9 (pbk.)

The point of view, opinions and conclusions expressed in this book are the author's. They serve as a basis for you to develop a landscape design, and they provide a starting point for the installation of your garden.

CONTENTS

ACKNOWLEDGMENTS

I am greatly indebted to Mom, Dad, Sandy and Jan for hours of thinking time and help above and beyond the call of family and friends.

Thank you Jim for the seed of an idea, and thank you Richard, without whom the seed would never have sprouted.

BIOGRAPHY

Joel Lerner was born in Flushing, New York, in 1947. At age 11 he began developing and maintaining neighbor's gardens. Since then, gardening has been a major part of his life. He has been involved with every aspect of plant design, installation and maintenance.

Joel is president of Environmental Design, a firm specializing in landscape contracting and design, with offices in Harrisburg, Pennsylvania; Chevy Chase, Maryland; and Sarasota, Florida.

Nicknamed the "Garden Guru," Joel's designs are used in teaching at the university level and by professional design companies nationwide. He has lectured at institutions such as George Washington University, University of Maryland and the Smithsonian Institution.

He created LERNSCAPING®, a unique concept of environmental design, matching people's personalities to their properties. He has also designed horticultural recreation programs to be used in parks and other public areas.

Here's What the Experts Say About Joel M. Lerner's
101 Townhouse Garden Designs:

"Urban gardeners need not despair."
The Washington Post

"Joel Lerner is waging war on wasted outdoor space."
Sarasota Herald Tribune

"At last there's a book for those who crave a green oasis in a pocket square of land."
The Washingtonian Magazine

"He combines teaching with design. It's like having your own personal tutor."
The Baltimore Sun

". . . (His) ideas are of such a wide diversity as to cover every situation imaginable."
The Journal

"The whole idea is to get people thinking and planning on their own."
The Harrisburg Patriot

LERN•SCAPE (lern' skāp) vt: to put you in touch with your property and make it reflect the essence of your personality.

INTRODUCTION

101 Townhouse Garden Designs is based upon 15 years of personal experience communicating landscaping expertise to property owners. This book serves as a means of advising you of the landscaping options for your townhouse property. There are an infinite number of design ideas to fit a property, but the best ideas are the ones that help you create a personalized design.

You are the best qualified person to decide what activities will take place in your garden and what "look" you want. For this reason I developed the LERNSCAPE® Design Concept. It is a simple process that puts you in touch with your property to make your garden reflect the essence of your personality. While some advice and help must come from experts, LERNSCAPING® translates your needs into a language that can be understood by the landscape architect, designer or nurseryman.

Part I contains a designer checklist, starting on page 12, consisting of over 80 considerations about your property, and puts you on the road to discovery. It provides the information you need to make decisions about your property that should be made before one nail is driven or a spade of soil is turned. Even if you intend to plant only one tree, planning will ensure that it is planted in the best location for the most value at maturity.

The checklist covers color, seasonal interest, energy efficiency, size, favorite plants, and many more ideas. Fill out the checklist to discover more about what you want for your property. This handy record will be a useful reference as you review the designs and develop your own plan.

Next, use the garden activity and style list on page 15 to guide you to the garden designs that fit your personality. Check the activities and styles that best describe how you wish to feel and what you want to do in your garden. Then flip to the pages that you have chosen in Part II, beginning on page 17, and review the designs, choosing those that fit your needs.

The designs are applicable for many uses. You should consider them carefully, noting your favorites. Thousands of combinations can be created by adding or eliminating elements and by putting whole or partial designs together. They are all drawn using the same scale to facilitate mixing and matching of designs.

Part III, starting on page 123, lists names of plants commonly sold in many parts of the country. This is by no means a definitive list and should serve only as a core for possibilities. See what others have done. Check out the gardens around the neighborhood. Visit public gardens, arboretums, conservatories and garden centers.

Don't skimp on ideas! LERNSCAPING® means getting involved with the planning of your property now, while it has only cost you thinking time. Photograph the design site; check the drainage; identify the most- and least-pleasant view; take measurements; note the compass points, and where and when the sun hits your property; test the soil; check soil depth and locate underground utilities. Following these steps now will save time and money in the future.

You are now ready to develop your design! Fill out the designer checklist and make your choice of garden designs. Use photos, site measurements and any other records you have compiled. Put your design choices together by cutting and pasting the designs onto a larger sheet of paper, making sure to include the ideas that you have compiled.

Now that you have a picture of what you want for your property, consult with a professional at your local garden center, and review your ideas. Such a person, with years of field experience and a background in horticulture, can make suggestions for the best plants and materials to suit your needs.

By following the LERNSCAPING® Design Concept, you will ensure that your outdoor living space will be a satisfying extension of your personality.

Joel M. Lerner

PART I
CHECKLISTS

The checklists provided in the following section should be the first step for LERNSCAPING® your property. When using the checklists, be sure to include your every whim or fancy. This section should serve as a catalyst to stimulate your ideas so that you will develop some general garden themes to fit your personality.

Checklist A—The designer checklist is easy to follow and written in a way to help you organize your ideas. Read through it, and fill in the areas that apply to you. Note the part of the list entitled Property Characteristics. These are points that you should consider throughout the entire job. Poor surface drainage or damaged underground utilities can create further complications and costs for the project. You may wish to seek professional advice from a local garden center as your plans progress.

Checklist B—The garden activity and style list is designed to help you decide what mood your garden should convey and what activities will take place there. Simply go through and check the categories that most closely match your desires for your property. Check any number of categories that you wish. Across from each activity or style are the page numbers where these designs are located.

Have fun, and remember, thinking time is "free." You don't have to be practical at this point!

CHECKLIST A. DESIGNER CHECKLIST

Design Style (Optional)
_____ Oriental
_____ English
_____ American Colonial
_____ Modern
_____ Other

Design Style
_____ Formal
_____ Informal
_____ Rectilinear
_____ Curvilinear
_____ Contemporary
_____ Rustic
_____ Other _____

Construction Material
_____ Wood
_____ Brick
_____ Concrete
_____ Slate
_____ Rock

Design Functions
Entertainment ☐ Yes ☐ No
_____Frequency
_____Number

Seating ☐ Yes ☐ No
_____Permanent
_____Temporary

Patio ☐ Yes ☐ No
_____Size
_____Const. Mat.

Accessories ☐ Yes ☐ No
_____Water
_____Lighting
_____Statuary

Other Structures ☐ Yes ☐ No
_____ Trellis
_____ Pergola/Arbor
_____ Gazebo
_____ Barbecue Grill
_____ Pool, Hot Tub, Spa
_____ Conservatory
_____ Other

Children ☐ Yes ☐ No
_____ Number
_____ Ages
_____ Playground/Entertainment

Interests
Athletic Activities _____
Nature Activities _____
Cultural Activities _____
Other Activities _____

Utility
_____ Pets
_____ Clothesline
_____ Firewood
_____ Service Area
_____ Storage Area
_____ Tool Shed
_____ Potting Shed
_____ Greenhouse
_____ Compost
_____ Parking
_____ Budget
_____ Other

Type of Plant Material
_____ Foliage Plants
_____ Flowering Plants
_____ Fragrant Plants
_____ Perennial Flowers
_____ Annual Flowers
_____ Bulbs
_____ Cut Flowers
_____ Vegetables
_____ Herbs
_____ Fruits
_____ Other

Use of Plant Material
_____ Privacy
_____ Noise Reduction
_____ Energy Efficiency
_____ Attract Wildlife
_____ Discourage Wildlife
_____ Aesthetics

Plant Preferences
Favorite _____
Unfavorite _____
_____Evergreen
_____Deciduous

Color Preferences _____

Season Preferences _____

Primary Times Garden Will Be Used _____

_____

Maintenance

_____ Do you plan to maintain the property yourself?

_____ How much time can you devote?

_____ What do you enjoy doing in the garden?

_____ What don't you enjoy doing in the garden?

Property Characteristics

Measurements of Design Area _____

Compass Pts. & Hrs. of Sun _____

Surface Drainage _____

Location of Underground Utilities _____

Pleasant Views _____

Features Worth Retaining _____

Unpleasant Views _____

Other Characteristics _____

CHECKLIST NOTES:

_____
_____
_____
_____
_____
_____
_____
_____
_____
_____
_____
_____
_____
_____
_____
_____
_____
_____
_____
_____
_____
_____
_____
_____

CHECKLIST B.
GARDEN ACTIVITY AND STYLE SHEET

PART II
101 DESIGNS

From the checklists you filled out, you have developed an idea of the sort of garden that you want. Did you consider even your wildest imagination? Now it is time to create the LERNSCAPE® Design for your property. Use the information from the designer checklist as you browse through your design choices.

You will find four designs in each activity/style category. Pick a design from each of your category choices. Your choice of designs should represent many of your responses from the designer checklist (for example, curved or straight lines; type of paving, flowers, shrubs or accessories; gardening activities; and so on).

STEP 1—Cut out your favorite designs. If you find one that you like exactly as it appears in the book, your search is over, and you can go on to the next step. Otherwise, mark the parts from each of the designs that you liked best. Cut them out and piece them together. Use the blank townhouse template at the end of this section. Make photocopies if you want extras. Thumb through the rest of the designs in the book. Experiment with designs by whiting out and working in your own original ideas. Hint: *Simplicity Is The Best Policy*. The design should not be too busy or utilize too many colors, plant varieties or different types of construction materials. Remember that these are small garden areas.

STEP 2—This is a good time to decide on some favorite plants that you would like to have in your environment. Visit public and private gardens and your local garden centers.

STEP 3—Make a copy of your final design ideas. Take this, the designer checklist, and your notes to a professional in the landscaping field. With expert advice you can decide your best plan of action for implementing the garden installation.

NOTE: To keep the artistic clarity of the designs, trees may be represented somewhat smaller than their mature size. Be sure to check the suggested maximum size of trees chosen for your garden. The garden center staff will help you to develop the very important maintenance program as well. All gardens must be maintained in order to achieve lasting beauty.

101 DESIGNS

A. VEGETABLE GARDENING

1. The Fruits of Your Labor

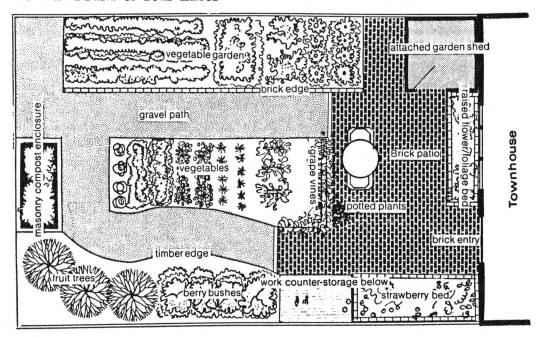

This garden is suited to both fruits and vegetables. Pick your straw-
berries fresh and treat yourself to breakfast on the patio.

2. Have Your Cake And Eat It Too

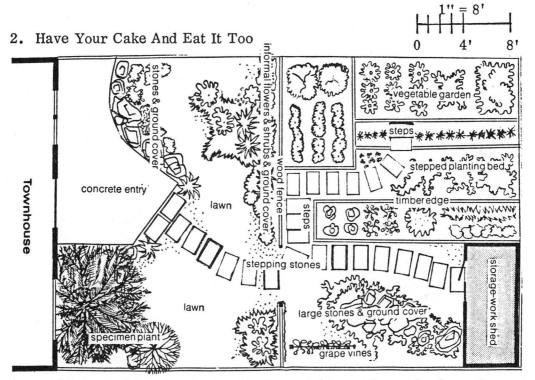

An aesthetic rock garden, a practical vegetable garden and a fence for privacy in either place.

A. VEGETABLE GARDENING

3. Expecting Company

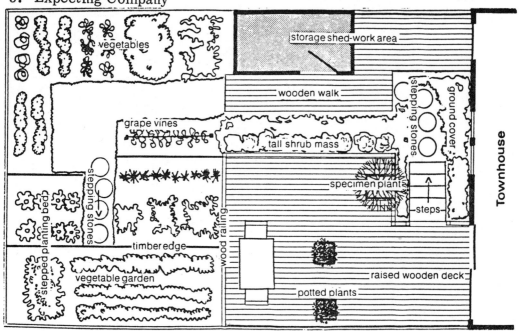

Entertain on the deck overlooking the garden, while you savor a fresh Caesar Salad and homemade vegetable soup.

4. Putter In The Garden

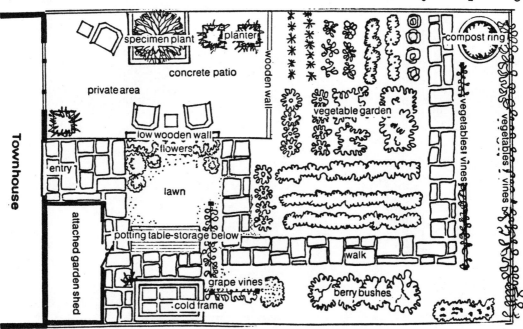

Everything for the avid vegetable gardener. There is even a place to sit and read the morning paper as you water the plants and watch your garden grow.

5. The Spice of Life

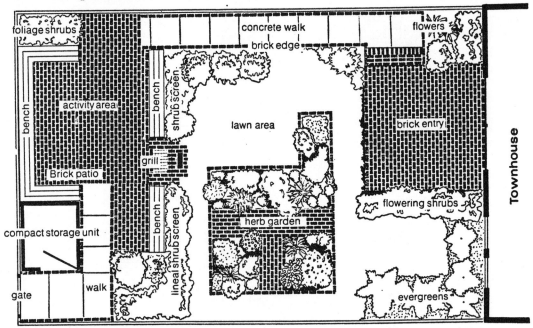

Herbs create a fine textured garden which is fragrant through the growing season, and provides seasoning throughout the year.

6. The Birds And The Bees

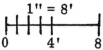

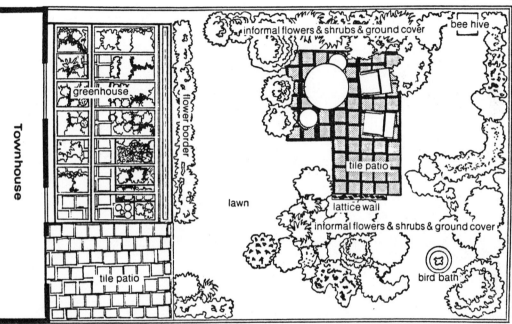

A ten by sixteen foot greenhouse will keep you busy year-round, and you can sit in the midst of your flowers and shrubs watching nature take its course.

B. FLOWER, SHRUB AND HERB GARDENING

7. The Garden of Eden

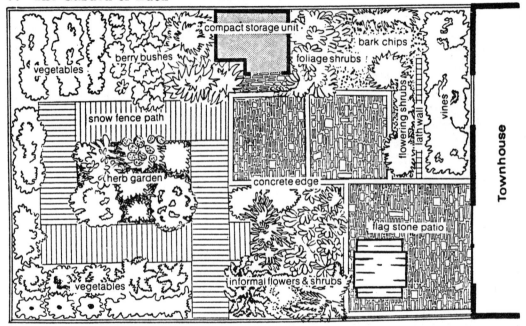

Put on your straw hat or bonnet, grab the garden basket and head for the great outdoors. The snow fence path and flagstone lend a rustic feel to your garden.

8. The Berry Patch

Scale: 1" = 8'
0   4'   8'

Townhouse

steps

wooden deck

decorative wood railing

low shrub mass

lawn

flowering shrubs

stones & ground cover

ground level wooden deck

garden shed

wooden walk

grape vines

grape vines

herb

strawberry bed

berry garden

berry bushes

foliage shrub

vines

Berries, as with all life, need the sun. Most plants that have been planted for yield will be more fruitful in sunny areas.

C. SUNNING

9. Don't Peek

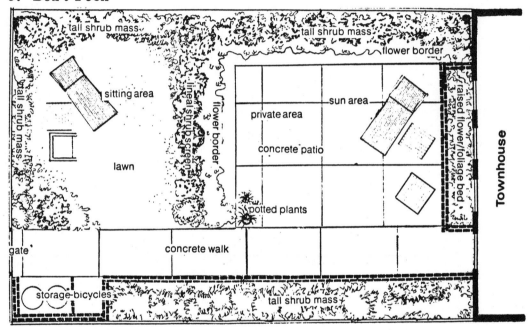

Privacy is the key consideration, and you get it. Surround yourself in color on your patio or sit in privacy on the back lawn.

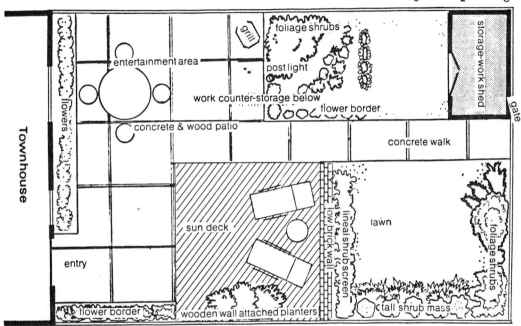

The patio provides an outdoor room for your family. The sun deck provides a quiet sitting area, or you can throw a towel down and bathe in privacy.

C. SUNNING

11. Different Levels of Entertainment

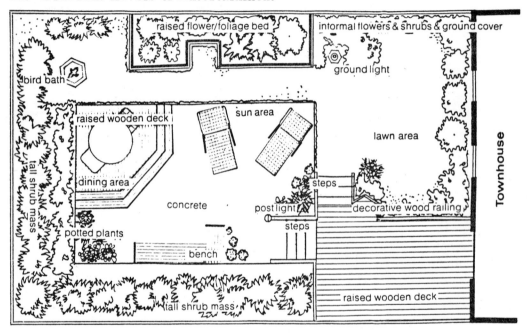

Sun yourself and have room to entertain guests. Use the patio, lawn and deck to add interest to any party.

12. Curves In All The Right Places

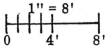

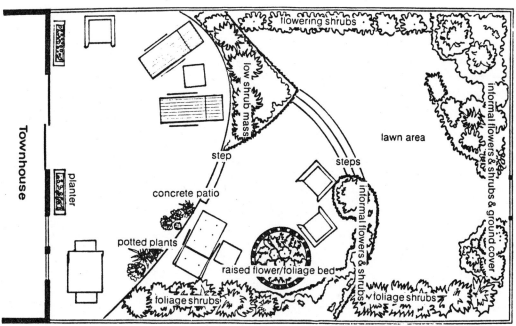

A modern, open and inviting garden for color and interest on all levels.

D. PETS AND YOUR GARDEN

13. Pets Are People Too

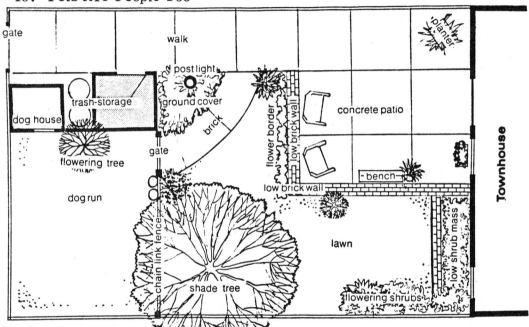

Set up for dog and family. Room to run on lawn and patio, and to give your pet a home of its own. Just remember, larger animals occasionally need more room to run than the townhouse garden will offer.

14. Close Knit Family

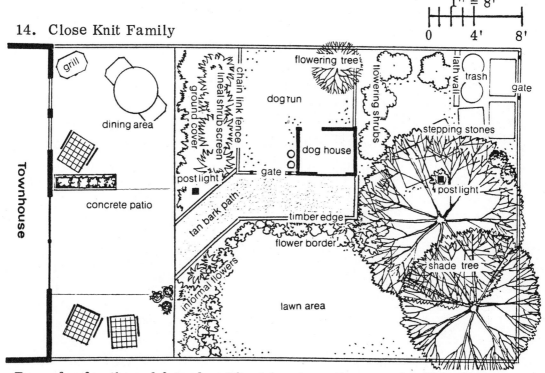

1" = 8'

0   4'   8'

Townhouse

grill

dining area

concrete patio

post light

chain link fence
lineal shrub screen
ground cover

tan bark path

informal flowers

flowering tree

dog run

dog house

gate

timber edge

flower border

lawn area

flowering shrubs

lath wall

trash

gate

stepping stones

post light

shade tree

Room for family and friends without leaving out your pet. This design puts your pet where the action is.

D. PETS AND YOUR GARDEN

15. It's A Dog's Life

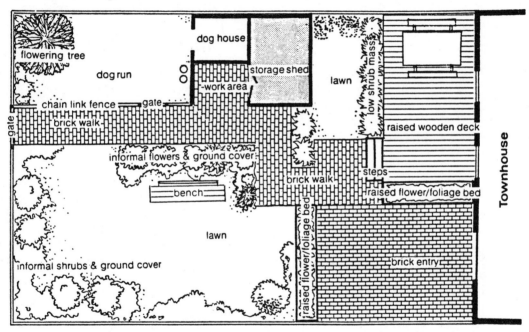

If you wish, give Fido free run of the garden. Low intensity planting should provide plenty of room for everybody. Consult your local garden center. There must be dog-proof plants!

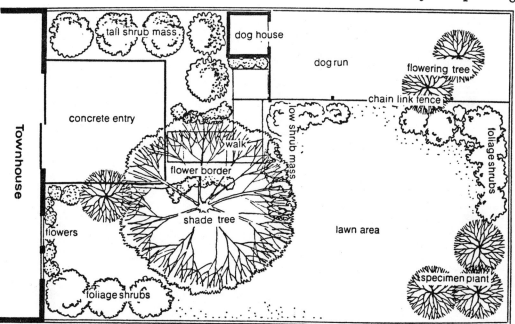

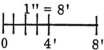

1" = 8'

0   4'   8'

Townhouse

tall shrub mass

dog house

dog run

flowering tree

concrete entry

chain link fence

low shrub mass

walk

flower border

foliage shrubs

shade tree

lawn area

flowers

specimen plant

foliage shrubs

Your dog has room to run on the lawn area and within the enclosure.
Please remember though, a town house garden provides limited running
area for any creature.

35

17. Keep The Home Fire Burning

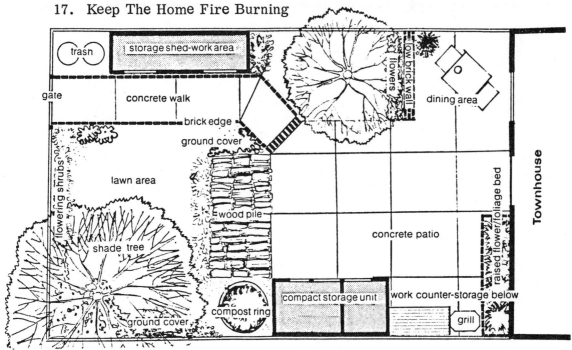

trash

storage shed-work area

gate

concrete walk

brick edge

ground cover

low brick wall

flowers

dining area

Townhouse

flowering shrubs

lawn area

wood pile

ground cover

shade tree

compost ring

concrete patio

raised flower/foliage bed

compact storage unit

work counter-storage below

grill

A stack of firewood creates a screen for a back semi-shaded lawn area, and there is lots of storage for axe and gardening tools.

18. No Shortage Of Storage

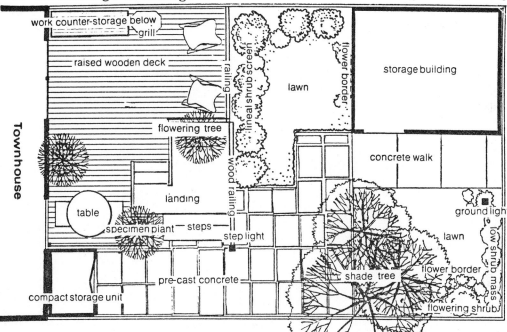

1" = 8'

0   4'   8'

work counter-storage below

grill

raised wooden deck

railing

lineal shrub screen

lawn

flower border

storage building

flowering tree

wood railing

concrete walk

Townhouse

landing

table

specimen plant — steps —

step light

ground light

shade tree

lawn

low shrub mass

pre-cast concrete

flower border

compact storage unit

flowering shrub

This garden is as utilitarian as they come, with beautiful outdoor living spaces, storage and work areas galore. Even store under the deck without sacrificing the looks of your garden.

37

19. Small Workshop For Small Projects

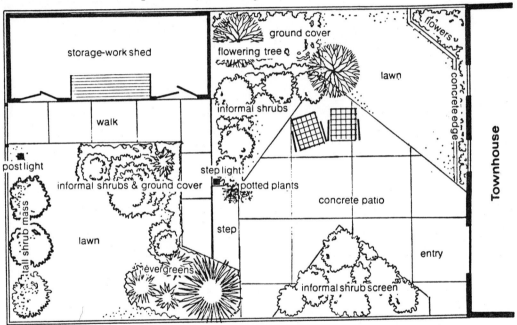

An area of modern beauty, with an out of the way shed and work bench for those projects that you can't do in the house.

20. Wall For Storage

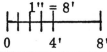

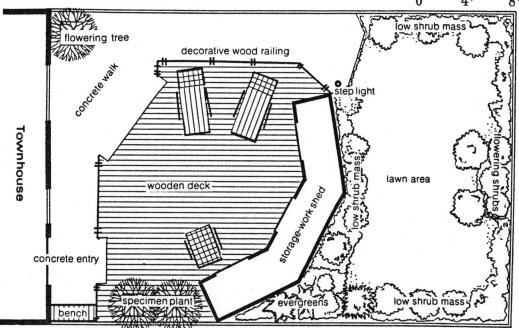

Storage becomes an added feature as this wooden storage shed serves as a room divider, creating a private deck as well as a private lawn area.

F. PRIVACY AND MEDITATION

21. Alone At Last!

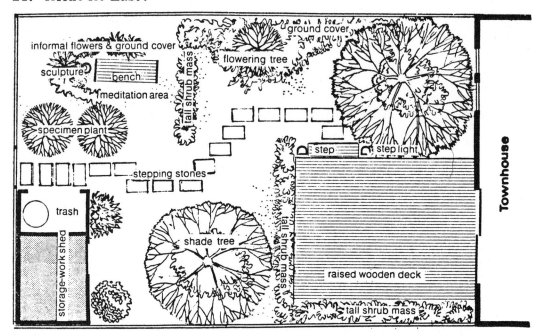

Use the deck for privacy, or during more quiet moments stroll through the garden, and be alone with your thoughts.

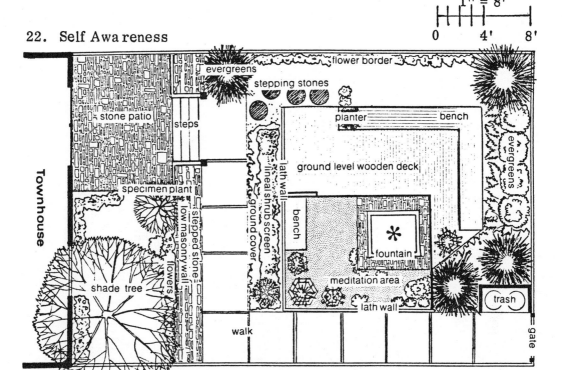

The center of the yard features an enclosed meditation area with fountain and two sitting areas. Get in touch with your feelings in this setting.

F. PRIVACY AND MEDITATION

23. Serenity

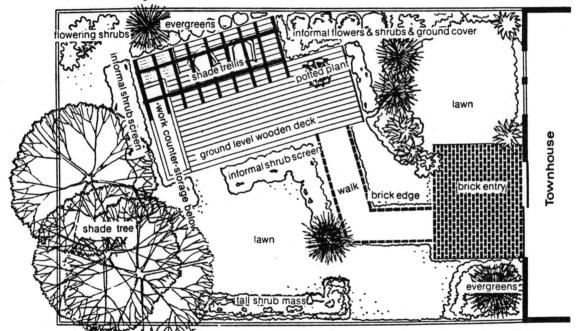

The trees offer a soothing, quiet feeling as you walk to the private deck. The classical brick entry blended with a modern deck and shade trellis offer a touch of the past and a touch of the present.

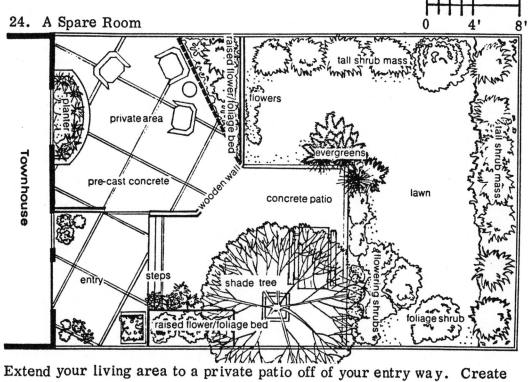

1" = 8'

0   4'   8'

Townhouse

planter

private area

pre-cast concrete

raised flower/foliage bed

wooden wall

flowers

tall shrub mass

evergreens

tall shrub mass

concrete patio

lawn

entry

steps

shade tree

flowering shrubs

raised flower/foliage bed

foliage shrub

Extend your living area to a private patio off of your entry way. Create a room with a view.

25. Enclosed From All But Nature

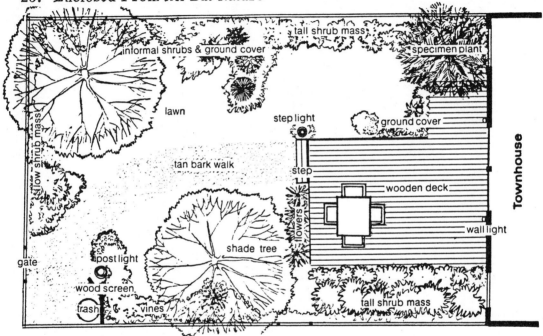

This rather simple design is spacious for your world within, yet well enclosed from the world without

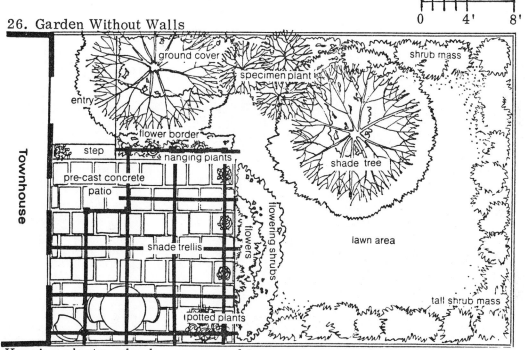

Labels within the drawing: 1" = 8', 0, 4', 8', ground cover, specimen plant, shrub mass, entry, flower border, step, hanging plants, pre-cast concrete, patio, shade tree, Townhouse, flowering shrubs, flowers, shade trellis, lawn area, tall shrub mass, potted plants

Hanging plants, shrub masses and trees ensure a private sitting area for relaxation. The trees will give a cool comfortable canopy come July.

27. A Keyhole Garden

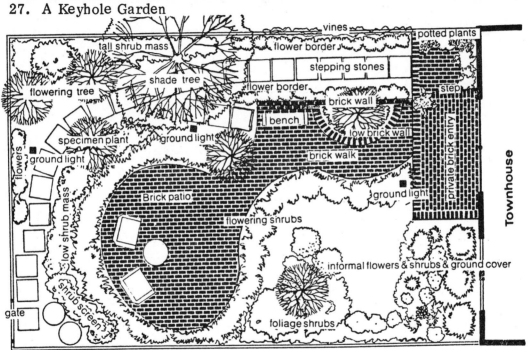

Walk into a splash of color which, if well coordinated, can create exitement through the growing season. This garden offers a sense of mystery and strong enclosure, as you pass the 6' brick wall and enter another world.

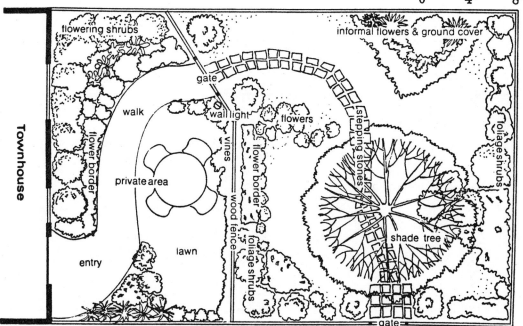

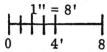

You will be tempted to hide in the privacy of your courtyard, but walk through the gates once in a while to behold your world around you.

29. Easy Living

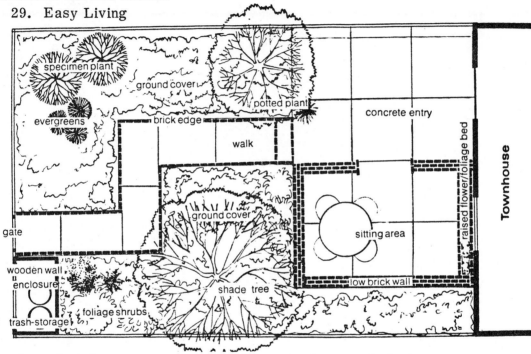

If you feel that your garden should be " the less work the better," plant a thick low growing ground cover and weeding chores will diminish. As your garden grows you will have more and more time to relax.

1" = 8'

0   4'   8'

foliage bed

low brick wall

gate

potted plant

dining area

work counter-storage below

grill

low brick wall

Townhouse

wall light

Brick patio

low brick wall

brick entry

evergreens

meditation area

foliage bed

storage bench

low brick wall

foliage bed

bench

Pave it, put in raised beds, plant slow growing shrubbery, and there you have it! Devote virtually no time maintaining your garden. Spend it instead enjoying the added room.

31. Too Busy To Bother

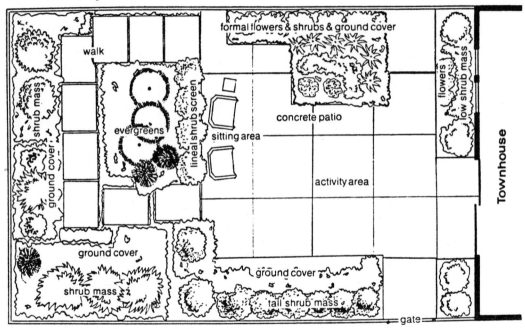

formal flowers & shrubs & ground cover

flowers

low shrub mass

Townhouse

walk

shrub mass

evergreens

lineal shrub screen

sitting area

concrete patio

ground cover

activity area

ground cover

shrub mass

ground cover

tall shrub mass

gate

No lawn to mow; lots of area for activities, and you'll still be surrounded by lush foliage.

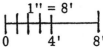

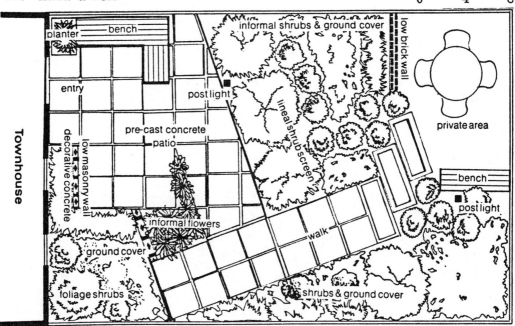

Concrete and shrubbery: inviting, informal and interesting. Be sure to use shrubs with a low maintenance requirement, and this unique patio arrangement will offer years of lasting beauty.

33. A Swinging Arrangement

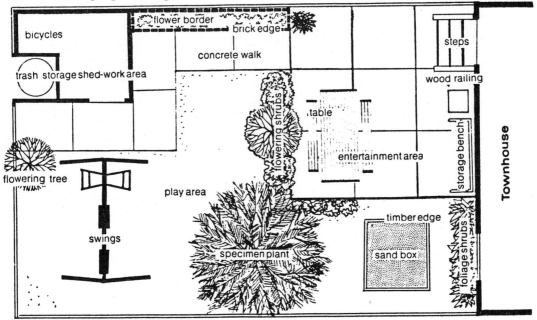

Swings and sandbox with storage for playthings. A great place for family picnics.

34. Rustic Beauty

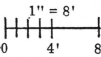

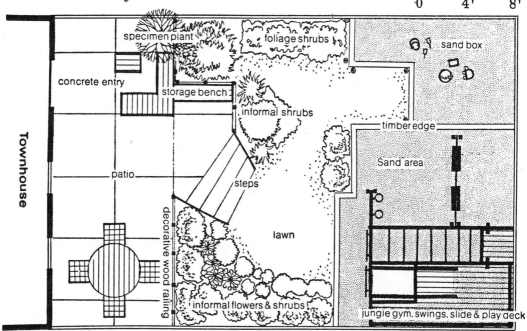

No need to sacrifice beauty for your children's needs. A rustic wooden playgym adds a nice touch to the landscape. Sit on the deck and keep the kids company.

I. KINDERGARDENS

35. No Generation Gap

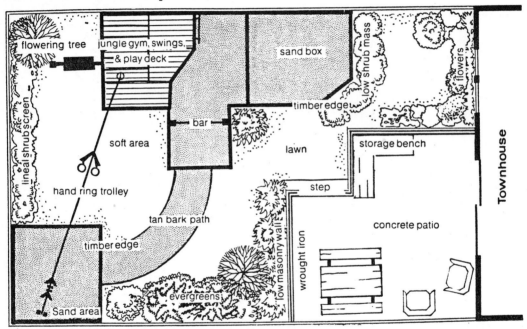

A decorative garden for mom and dad and a playground that would be fun for the whole family offers something for everyone.

36. Daycare

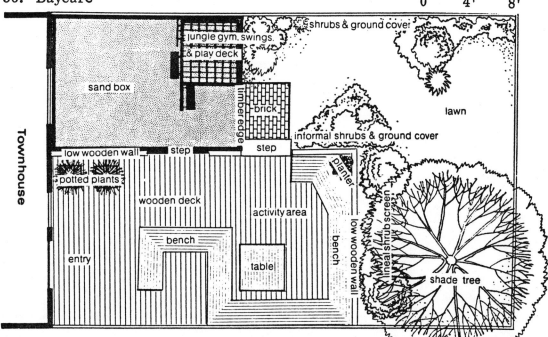

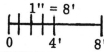

1" = 8'

0   4'   8'

Townhouse

shrubs & ground cover

jungle gym, swings, & play deck

sand box

timber edge

brick

lawn

informal shrubs & ground cover

low wooden wall   step   step

potted plants

wooden deck   planter

activity area

bench

lineal shrub screen

low wooden wall   bench

entry

table

shade tree

This garden keeps the kids close where you can see them, and it provides lots of open area for serving lunches and snacks, taking naps, ball playing, somersaulting, diaper changing, jumping, digging, ...

37. Dance, Dance, Dance

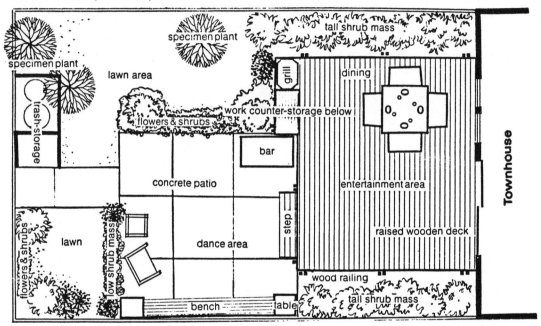

A large entry deck with adjoining patio creates a spacious atmosphere. Two lawn areas provide an opportunity to steal away and make that new acquaintance.

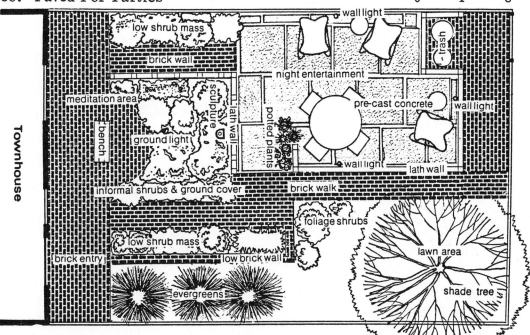

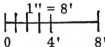

The brick and concrete patios blend to create a contemporary – colonial look. Intensive paving offers lots of room. The interspersed planting beds lend softness to the overall design, and the enclosed sitting area is conducive to intimate conversation.

39. Garden Party

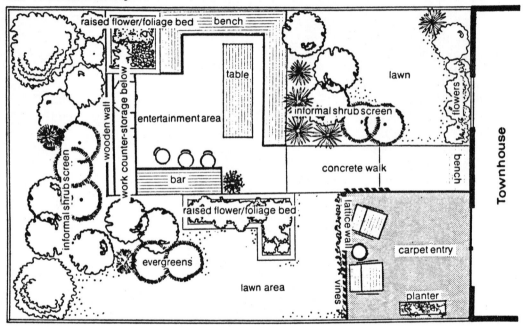

A showy display of shrubbery is the perfect touch for a successful afternoon lawn party. The paved area will accommodate a bar and serving area.

40. The Multi-Purpose Room

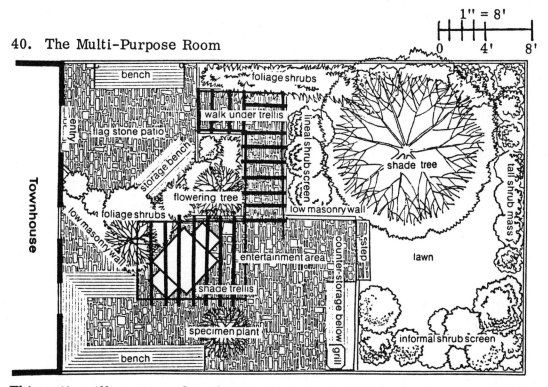

This patio will accommodate dances, games, meetings, barbeques, clam-bakes and more. Use your imagination. The pergola, trellis and large tree create an enclosed sociable atmosphere.

41. All Decked Out

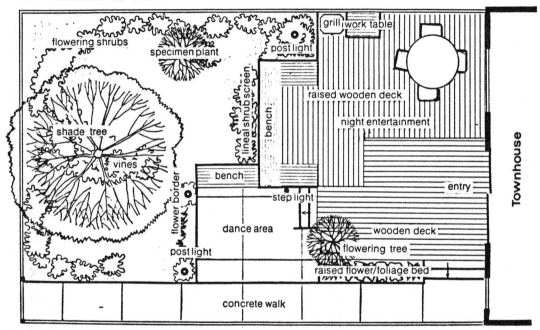

With generous seating and space for dancing, this garden is planned for action. Lawn, trees and shrubbery create the perfect background for an evening on the terrace.

42. Autumn Breeze

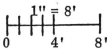

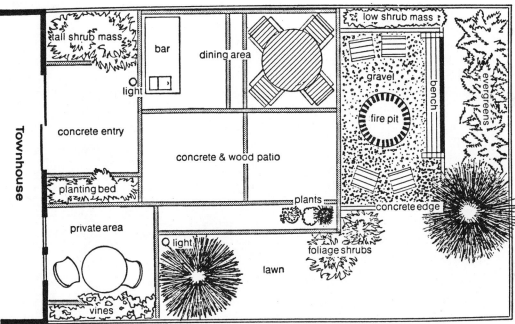

Special friends and a cool autumn evening will transform your garden into a magical place. Firepit, bar and dining area are the perfect complements to an evening in the garden.

43. Bacchanalia

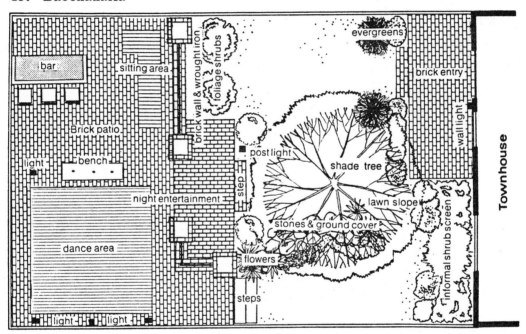

Everything you need for a successful evening's get together. Dance, talk, drink and eat in your own personal nightclub. Enjoy the night air in style.

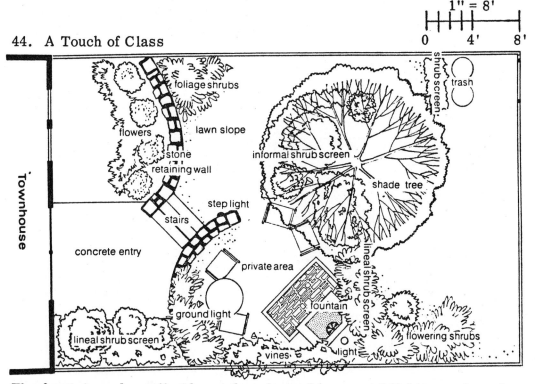

1" = 8'

0   4'   8'

foliage shrubs

flowers

lawn slope

stone
retaining wall

informal shrub screen

shade tree

Townhouse

step light

stairs

concrete entry

private area

ground light

shrub screen

trash

lineal shrub screen

fountain

lineal shrub screen

flowering shrubs

vines

light

The fountain and small side yard, enhanced by ground lighting and garden wall, make a cozy spot to sit and visit. Your guests will get an extra treat when plants are in bloom.

45. Country Garden

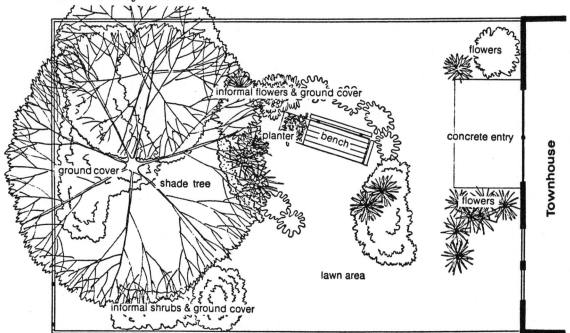

The sweeping free formed bed line and perennial flowers will give you the feeling of strolling through a meadow filled with wild flowers. This feeling is conveyed by many English estate gardens throughout the English country-side.

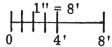

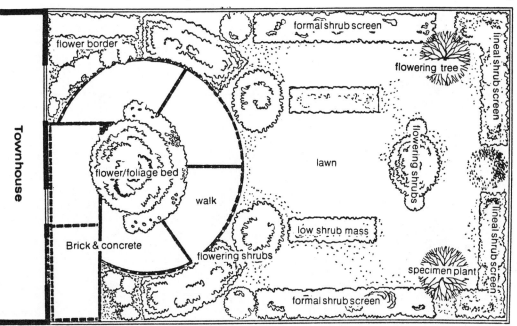

As you exit your townhouse, a treat lies hidden beyond the shrubs. You enter the garden and feel as if you have walked into a castle courtyard. Remember though, intensive pruning is required.

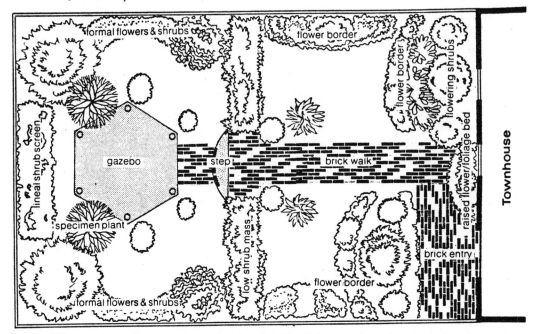

You will create a flowery wonderland with this garden design, but keep in mind that weeding and pruning are important for lasting beauty.

48. Five O'Clock Tea

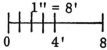

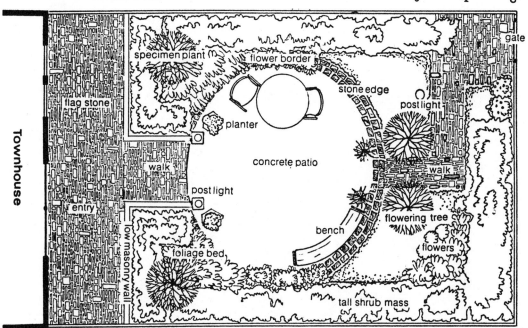

A naturalistic English country patio features abundant shrubs and perennials.
The paved areas lower the maintenance requirements for this garden.

49. Eastern Philosophy

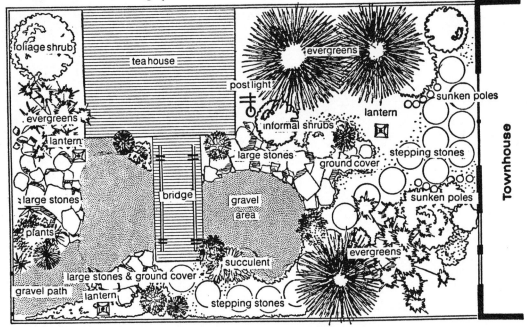

Walk out your back door into luxurious simplicity. The symbolic use of plants and structures make this garden a Japanese experience. Follow the stone path through the forest, past the river and over the bridge to arrive at your mountain retreat.

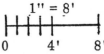

1" = 8'

0   4'   8'

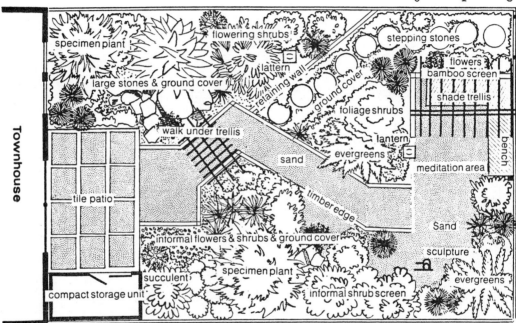

Townhouse

specimen plant

flowering shrubs

stepping stones

flowers

bamboo screen

lattern

large stones & ground cover

retaining wall

ground cover

shade trellis

foliage shrubs

walk under trellis

lantern

evergreens

sand

meditation area

bench

tile patio

timber edge

Sand

sculpture

informal flowers & shrubs & ground cover

evergreens

succulent

specimen plant

compact storage unit

informal shrub screen

A treat awaits you partially hidden behind lush shrubbery. Focal points
in the garden are revealed as you walk through and discover them. Sit
in the bamboo enclosure concealed from people, but in full view of nature.

51. Simplicity

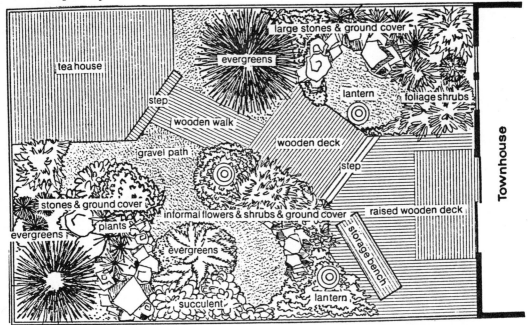

Wooden walks carry you across the lake through bountiful greenery. Arriving at your destination, serve tea and rice cakes. For authenticity, sit on woven mats.

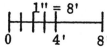

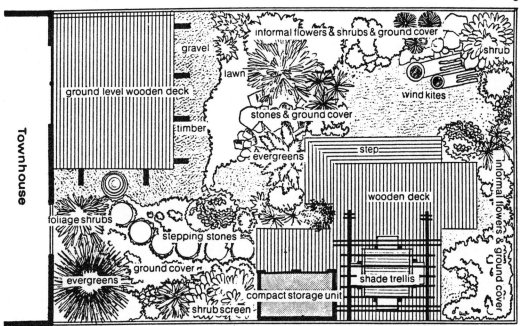

Entertain in your garden in kimono. Sip saki, meditate or simply visit with friends. With two decks from which to view the landscape, you will find a lot of variety in your garden.

53. Somewhat Formal

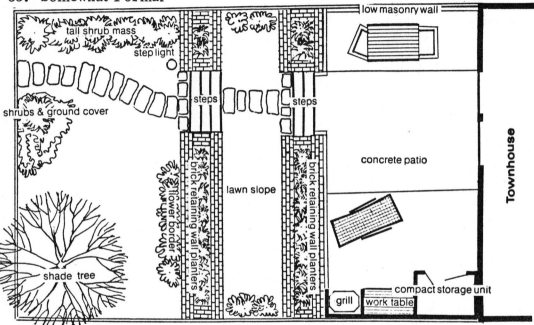

Formalize your sloped area with straight retaining walls, level lawn areas and lineal rows of plants. Meandering stone path and a medium to large tree soften the picture.

54. Mixed Media

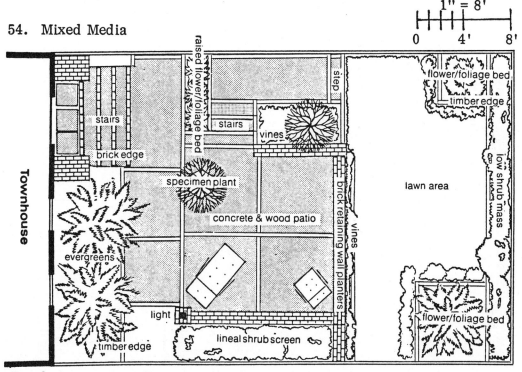

1" = 8'

0   4'   8'

Townhouse

raised flower/foliage bed

stairs

brick edge

specimen plant

stairs

vines

concrete & wood patio

evergreens

light

timber edge

lineal shrub screen

step

brick retaining wall planters

vines

lawn area

flower/foliage bed

timber edge

low shrub mass

flower/foliage bed

Brick, concrete and wood make a tastefully smooth transition from an all brick townhouse down into a contemporary garden. Whether you use a low or tall shrub mass at the end of the yard will depend upon the view and the degree of privacy that you desire.

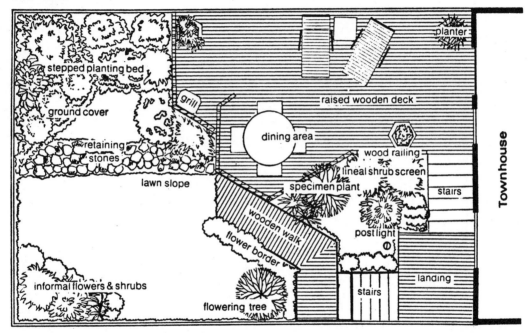

Slopes offer the opportunity to add another dimension of interest. Plants which are viewed from above take on a new character as you descend into the garden and see them from another plane.

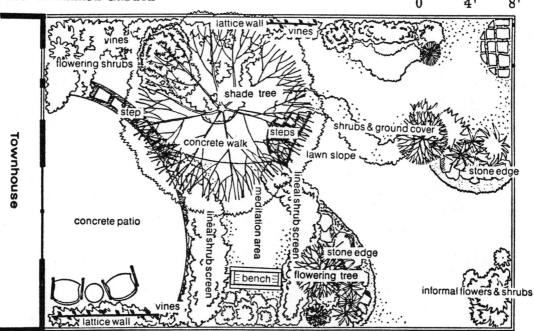

1" = 8'

0   4'   8'

Townhouse

lattice wall
vines
vines
flowering shrubs
step
shade tree
shrubs & ground cover
concrete walk
steps
lawn slope
stone edge
meditation area
lineal shrub screen
lineal shrub screen
concrete patio
stone edge
flowering tree
bench
informal flowers & shrubs
vines
lattice wall

The curvilinear design makes this landscape flow from your patio into the rest of your property. As you descend the stone steps, the adjoining terraces will make perfect rock gardens.

57. A Variety Of Perspectives

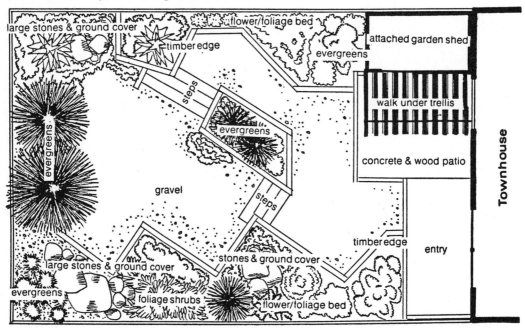

Timbers jut in and out of planting beds, and steps run at opposite angles to each other providing many perspectives from which to view your garden. Of course, the best part is that there's no lawn to mow!

58. Envelope Garden

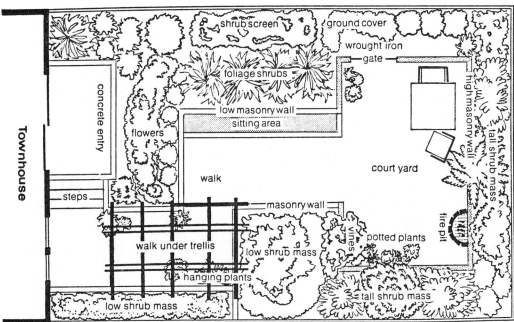

Scale: 1" = 8'   0'   4'   8'

(Garden plan labels: Townhouse, concrete entry, flowers, steps, walk, walk under trellis, low shrub mass, hanging plants, shrub screen, foliage shrubs, low masonry wall, sitting area, ground cover, wrought iron gate, high masonry wall, tall shrub mass, court yard, masonry wall, vines, potted plants, fire pit, low shrub mass, tall shrub mass)

For complete privacy, a 6' concrete wall surrounds the courtyard. To soften the picture, foliage in the bed behind the wall can be trained to cascade or climb on it. A low garden wall leads from the house, giving continuity to the design.

O. GARDENS WITHOUT LAWNS

59. A Natural Setting

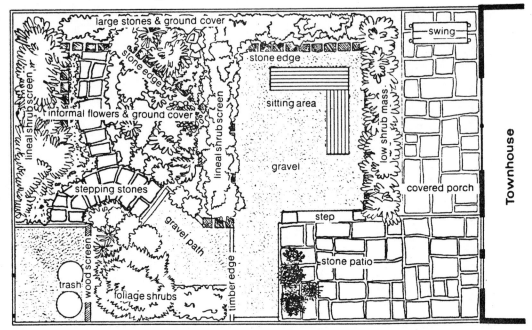

A permanent patio makes a clean entranceway and creates an area for permanent seating. The gravel and stone paths invite you to visit the garden, and experience it with all of your senses for all of the seasons.

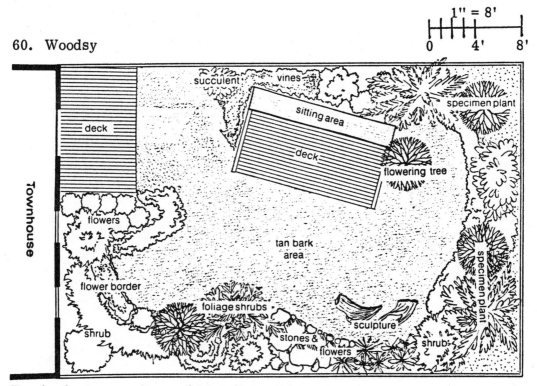

1" = 8'

0   4'   8'

Townhouse

deck

succulent   vines

sitting area

deck

specimen plant

flowering tree

flowers

tan bark
area

specimen plant

flower border

foliage shrubs

sculpture

shrub

stones &
flowers

shrub

Tan bark gives a clean, 'forest floor' appearance to your property. Simply
rake up the winter debris, spread a little fresh tan bark and enjoy the soft,
low maintenance area all season long.

61. Brick 'n Lawn

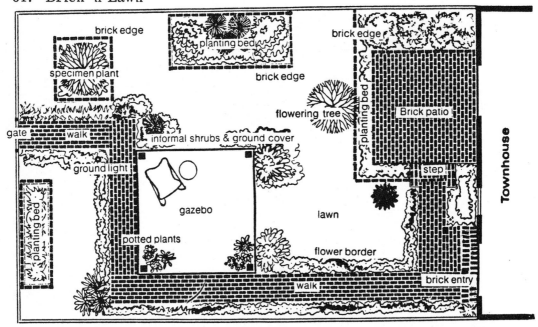

Brick patio, walks and edging set the theme for this garden, and a wooden gazebo adds a distinctive touch. Sit and while the hours away amidst green lawn and foliage.

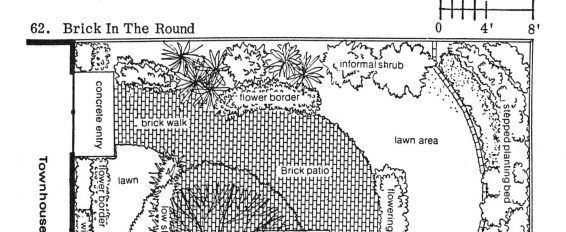

1" = 8'

0   4'   8'

Labels within figure:
Townhouse
concrete entry
flower border
window planter
lawn
brick walk
flower border
low shrub mass
shade tree
table
Brick patio
flowering shrubs
lawn area
informal shrub
stepped planting bed
brick edge

This unique patio shape surrounded by flowering shrubs creates an intimate outdoor living space. The tree and stepped planting bed create a strong enclosure to complete the design.

63. Brick 'n Greenery

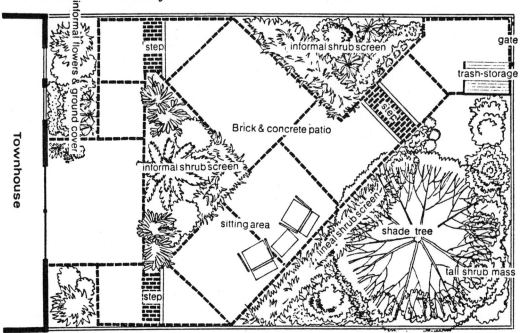

informal flowers & ground cover

step

Townhouse

informal shrub screen

gate

trash-storage

Brick & concrete patio

s.dec.

informal shrub screen

linear shrub screen

sitting area

shade tree

tall shrub mass

step

Brick accents lend a pleasing finished look to the concrete paving, while triangular planting beds bring lush green foliage in close to the sitting area.

64. Brick

1" = 8'
0   4'   8'

- vines
- flowering shrubs
- storage bench
- flowering tree
- post light
- private area
- post light
- informal shrub
- specimen plant
- sitting area
- lawn
- vines
- Brick patio
- bird bath
- Townhouse
- brick entry
- flowering shrubs
- vines
- brick wall fence

There's enough brick patio to satisfy the most avid brick buff. If that's not enough, the brick garden wall should do it. Remember, when paving surfaces, drainage considerations are critical.

65. Making Waves

An in-ground hot tub and an overlooking deck create a recreational retreat from which you will derive hours of pleasure. Careful, it may be habit-forming.

66. Creature Comforts

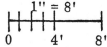

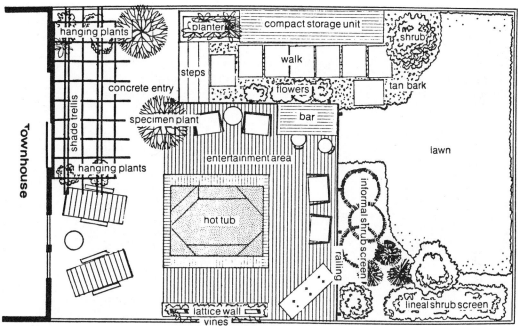

This modern design includes an inclosed relaxation area, a lawn area, storage and a hot tub complete with entertainment facilities. Don't count on friends or relatives to leave early.

Q. HOT TUB

67. Essentially Brick

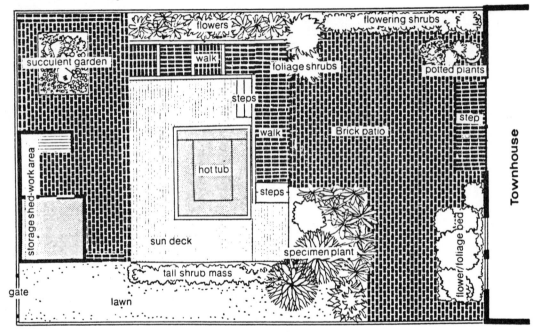

Obviously, the motif of this garden is brick, but the central focus is the raised wooden hot tub deck with matching storage shed/work area. Low maintenance adds an extra plus to this design.

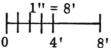

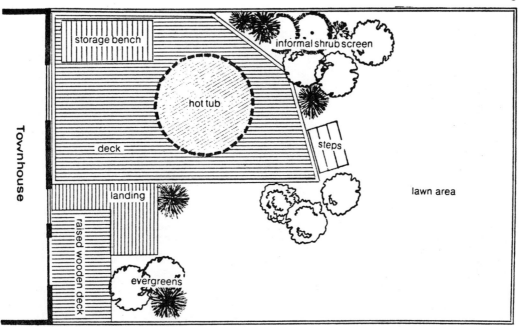

storage bench

informal shrub screen

hot tub

deck

steps

Townhouse

landing

lawn area

raised wooden deck

evergreens

An open design that's covered in all the right places. Plant shrubbery for screening that has a low maintenance requirement, and you'll barely need to worry about caring for your garden.

69. Digging the Soil

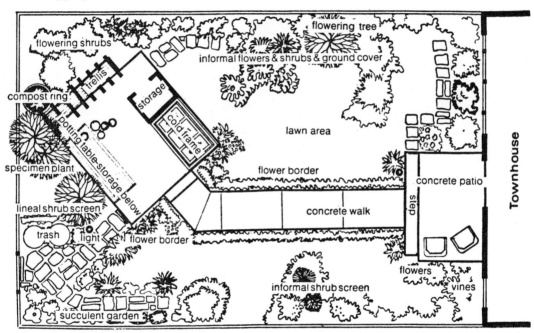

Labels within the plan:
flowering tree
flowering shrubs
informal flowers & shrubs & ground cover
trellis
storage
compost ring
cold frame
lawn area
potting table-storage below
specimen plant
flower border
Townhouse
lineal shrub screen
concrete patio
concrete walk
step
trash
light
flower border
flowers
informal shrub screen
vines
succulent garden

This design is custom made for plant lovers who like to do-it-themselves.
Cold frame, potting table, storage, compost area and lots of garden spaces
are provided.

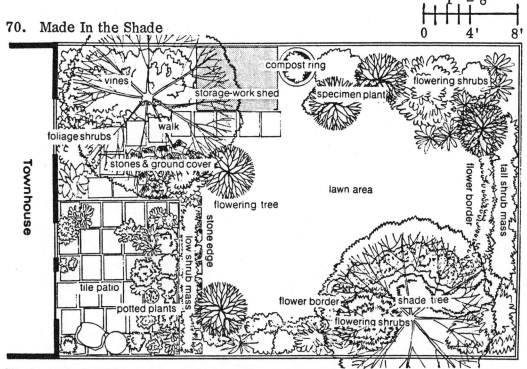

1" = 8'

0   4'   8'

compost ring

vines

storage-work shed

specimen plant

flowering shrubs

foliage shrubs

walk

stones & ground cover

Townhouse

flowering tree

lawn area

flower border

tall shrub mass

stone edge

low shrub mass

tile patio

potted plants

flower border

shade tree

flowering shrubs

Shade and shrubbery present a pretty picture together and create an intimate and rustic enclosure. Container plants for planting your patio bring the garden right into your home.

71. A Veritable Showplace

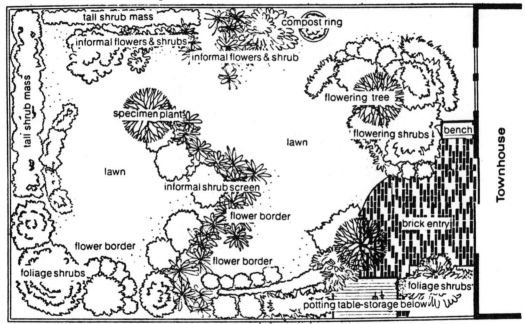

An informal shrub line extends into the center of the lawn to add interest and create a divider to add an extra dimention to the garden. Areas for many plants and a place for potting and storage are provided for plant collectors.

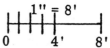

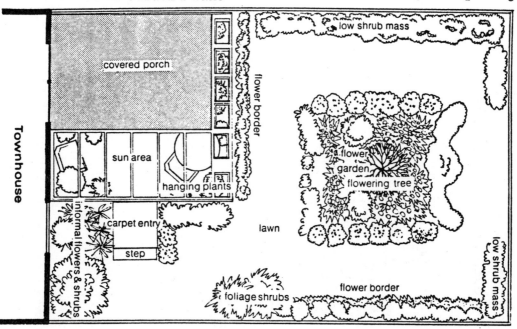

You will want to spend hours in your garden all year round. The covered porch, skylight and plants (inside and outside) create an hospitable atmosphere for even the least outdoor oriented individual. For added interest stagger flowering times throughout the growing season.

73. Multi-Functional

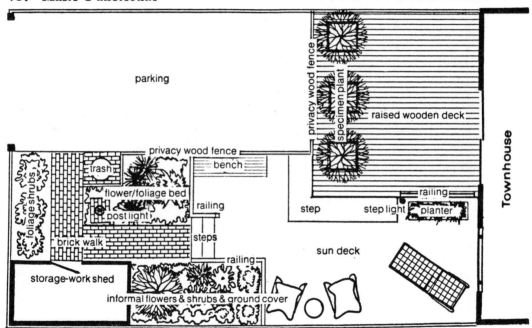

Enter your home through the garden. The design is organized for maximum plant, parking, patio and storage space. This design enables you to do it all. The only thing missing is a hot tub!

74. Kiss and Ride

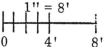

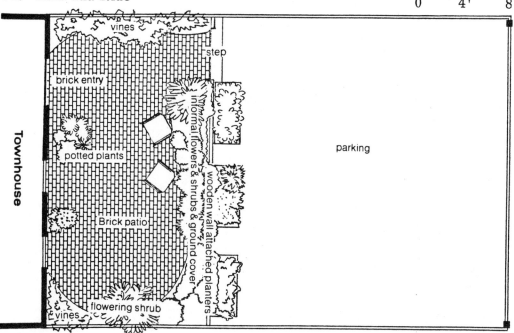

vines

step

brick entry

Townhouse

potted plants

informal flowers & shrubs & ground cover

wooden wall attached planters

Brick patio

parking

flowering shrub

vines

This patio, surrounded by flowers and greenery, creates a romantic setting in which to kiss your spouse as you depart for work. A carport and hanging planters make a practical addition for privacy on your patio

75. Cozy Spaces

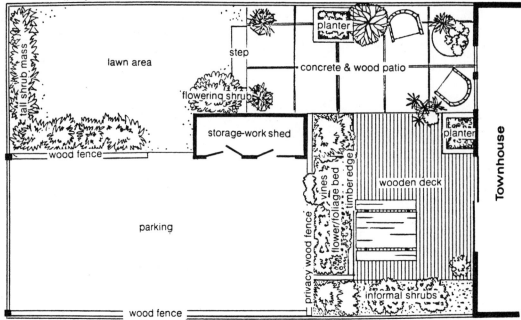

This design offers ample area for private dining and visiting. The lawn lends a spaciousness to the patio and creates a scenic entrance from the car.

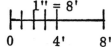

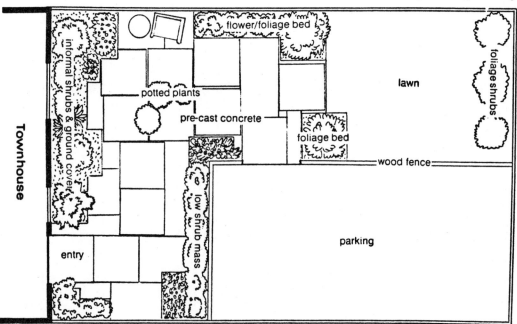

1" = 8'

0   4'   8'

flower/foliage bed

foliage shrubs

lawn

informal shrubs & ground cover

potted plants

pre-cast concrete

foliage bed

wood fence

Townhouse

low shrub mass

entry

parking

This garden gives you the feeling that you could afford a chauffeur.
Concrete and greenery are blended to give a prosperous, comfortable
and contemporary look.

95

77. Comfortable and Convenient

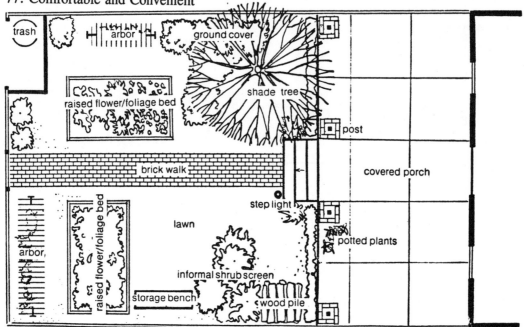

This is the way it may have looked then. There's no reason it can't be that way again. All the elements are here for an inviting and practical garden.

78. Prim and Proper

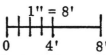

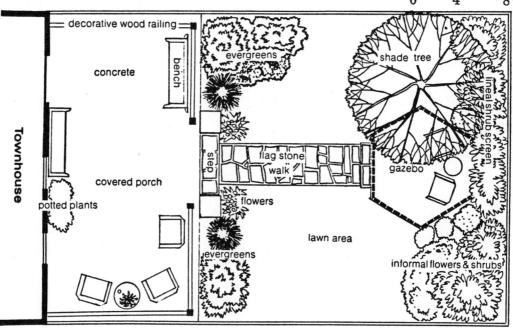

decorative wood railing

evergreens

shade tree

concrete

bench

lineal shrub screen

Townhouse

covered porch

flag stone walk

gazebo

step

potted plants

flowers

lawn area

evergreens

informal flowers & shrubs

Privacy, shade and quaintness best describe this garden. The gazebo adds a doll house look when viewed from the back porch.

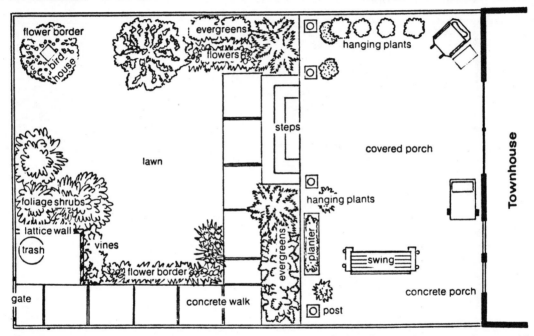

The seating and large porch are reminiscent of the days when people would sit out and visit with neighbors and friends. Recreate this hospitable atmosphere.

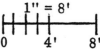

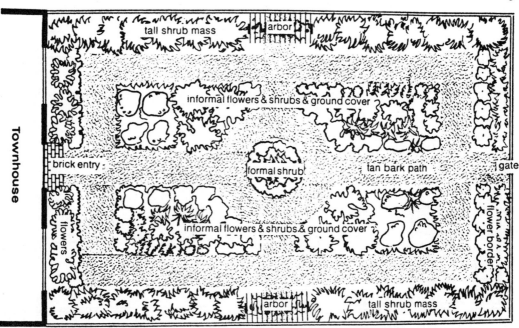

Perennials are gaining popularity lately. There are many varieties that would give color to this garden throughout the growing season. Tall shrubs give a soft enclosure to your private formal garden.

81. Sculpture Garden

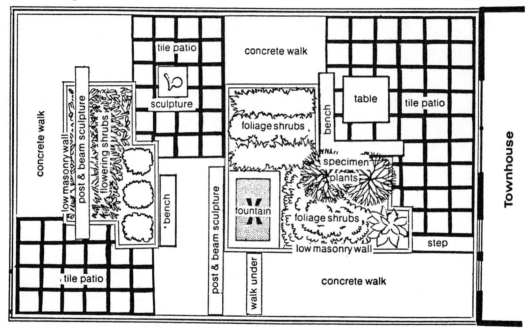

Overhead concrete beams and concrete support posts are important elements to the contemporary look. Beams, fountain and sculpture bend to create modern art.

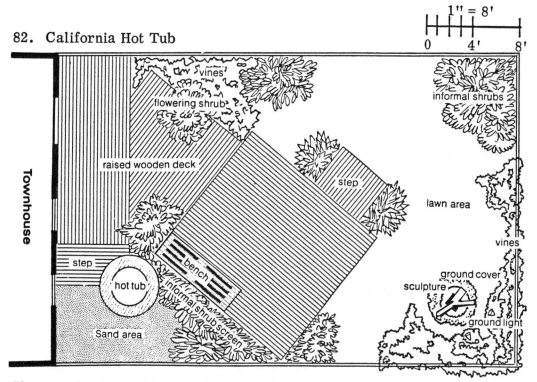

1" = 8'

0 4' 8'

Townhouse

vines

flowering shrub

informal shrubs 2

raised wooden deck

step

lawn area

vines

step

bench

ground cover

sculpture

hot tub

informal shrub screen

ground light

Sand area

Changing horizontal lines take you from one deck to another, defining the space for the hot tub. From the large central deck you can sun yourself as you enjoy modern sculpture and lush green shrubbery.

83. 2010

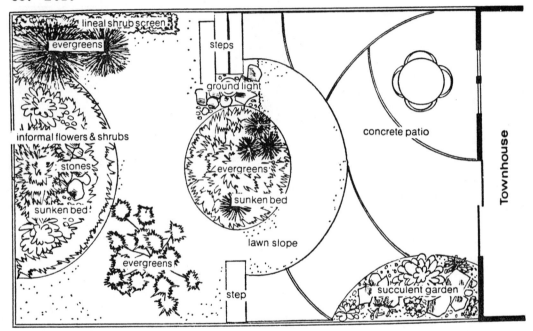

The lines of this garden are futuristic. Be sure to choose plants from another planet.

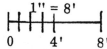

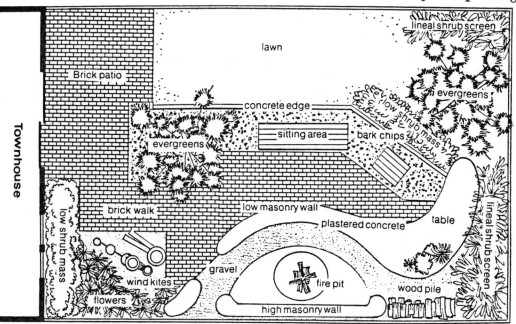

The rectangular brick patio blends with the flowing free form concrete accessories. Shrubbery, flowers and colorful windkites aid in the transition from classical to daring.

85. Rose-Colored Glasses

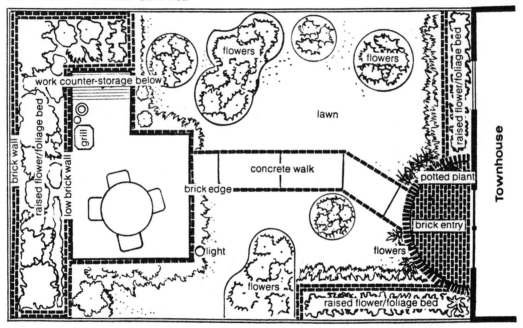

Roses and brick are commonly used together. Roses come in many colors, are aromatic and can be kept flowering all summer long, but they are a high maintenance plant. Pruning, diseases and insects may discourage you from planting all roses.

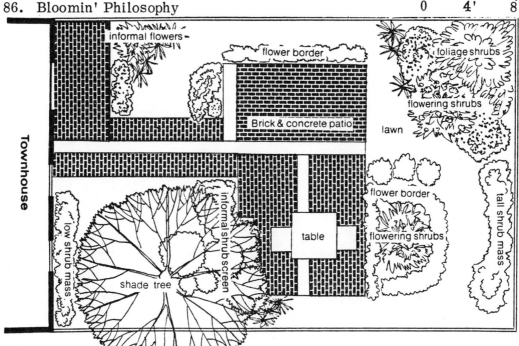

1" = 8'

0   4'   8'

informal flowers

flower border

foliage shrubs

flowering shrubs

Brick & concrete patio

lawn

Townhouse

low shrub mass

informal shrub screen

table

flower border

flowering shrubs

tall shrub mass

shade tree

Flowers console, show affection, cheer and soothe. They are a beautiful reminder of one of the most wondrous similarities between all life — procreation. Surround yourself with blooms.

V. FRAGRANCE WITH FLOWERS

87. Floramania

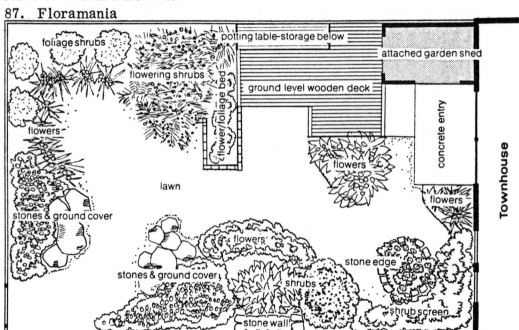

The shrubbery, perennials and annuals in your garden can be coordinated to flower continuously. Your property can be covered by a rainbow almost year round.

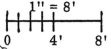

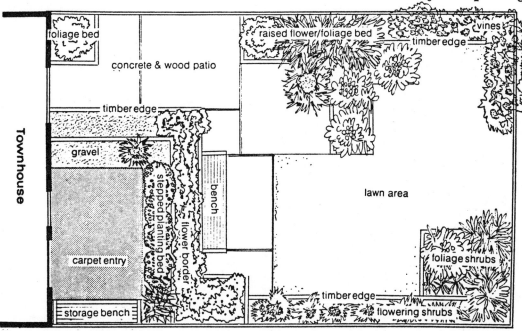

There are many flowering shrubs — some may be kept flowering throughout the growing season, some offer fragrance, some may be cut and taken indoors for decoration. Visit your local garden center and decide on the perfect flowers for your needs.

89. Right At Home

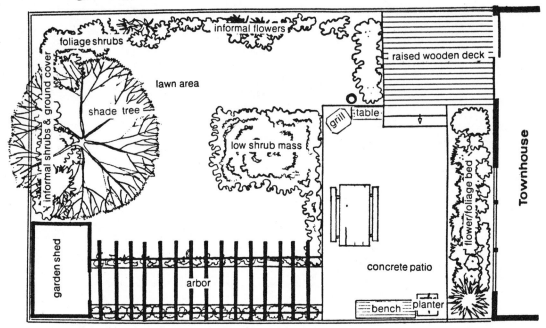

The arbor gives a cozy feel. The shade tree provides further enclosure, making this garden conducive to comfort and ease.

90. Laid Back

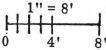

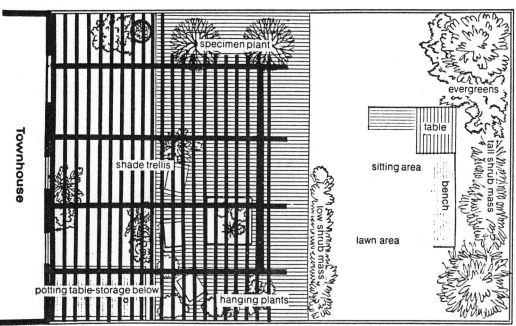

Sit in the garden or on the deck. The shade trellis sets the lazy mood.
Pipe out some mellow music and relax.

W. ARBORS FOR PLANTS OR OUTDOOR ROOMS

91. Open and Closed

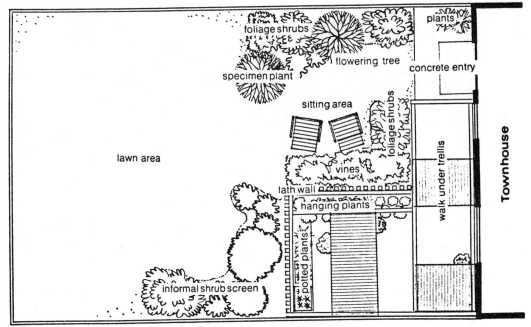

Use the shaded, walled in area to tinker with interior plants, or decorate with them to create a private retreat from the world.

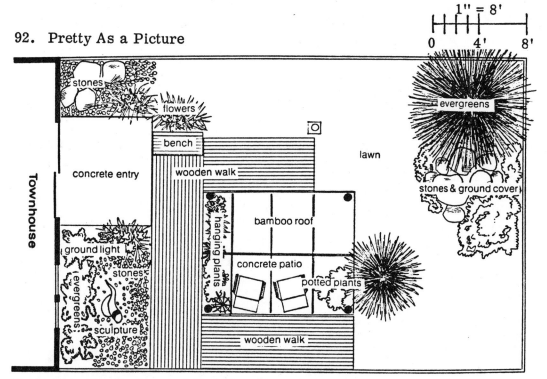

Patio is centrally located in order to experience the garden from all sides. Enjoy the arrangement of rocks, plants and sculpture. The bamboo roof is an aesthetic complement to this garden.

93. A Good Impression

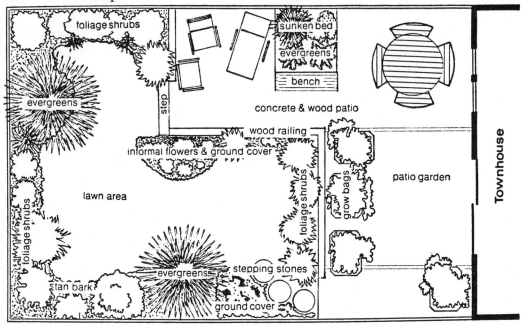

Seal that big deal, and do it in the privacy of your own home. Design your garden to double as an area for conducting business.

94. Fine Tuning

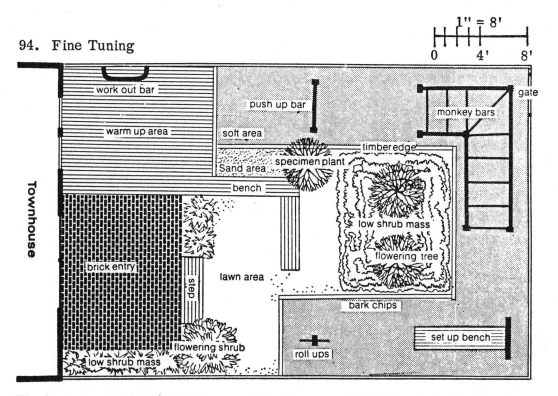

1" = 8'

0   4'   8'

work out bar

warm up area

push up bar

soft area

gate

monkey bars

timber edge

specimen plant

Sand area

bench

low shrub mass

flowering tree

Townhouse

brick entry

step

lawn area

bark chips

flowering shrub

low shrub mass

roll ups

set up bench

Workout in style. It could be good business to fine tune physically as you enjoy your tastefully decorated garden.

95. 9 to 5

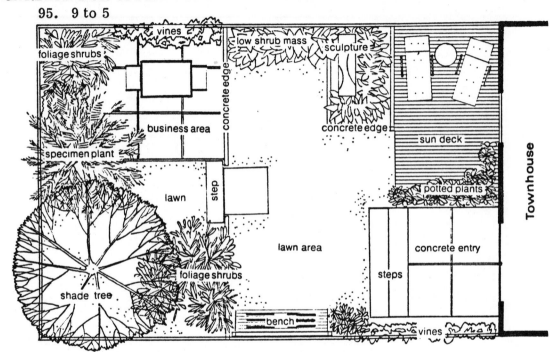

This is all the farther you need to travel from home. In these days of remote control and home computers, your garden could be a fair weather tax deduction.

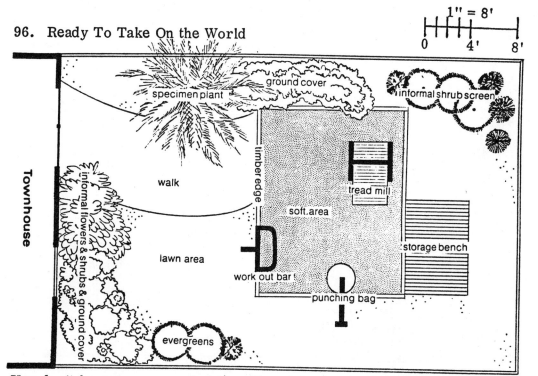

1" = 8'

0   4'   8'

Townhouse

specimen plant

ground cover

informal shrub screen

informal flowers & shrubs & ground cover

walk

timber edge

tread mill

soft area

lawn area

storage bench

work out bar

punching bag

evergreens

You don't have to worry what time the club opens, if the facilities are available or whether you will have the time. Just do it — right in your own back yard!

97. Reflections

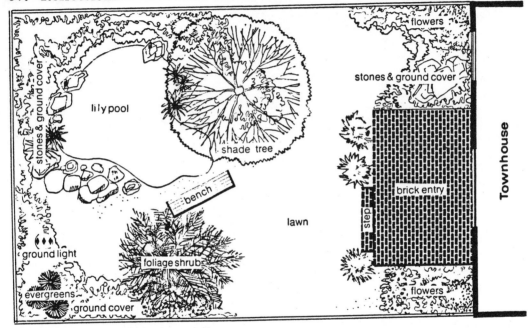

A free form lily pond is a peaceful addition to any garden, and reflections from the pool surface adds to the design. Remember, you also add to the maintenance.

98. Free Flowing

1" = 8'

0   4'   8'

Townhouse

shrub mass · informal shrub screen · tall shrub mass

flowers

flowering shrubs · flower border

lawn area

fountain

flowers & shrubs

tile patio

shade tree

tall shrub mass

Cascading water keeps bringing your attention back, and flowering plants make colorful splashes to complete this pastoral scene. Together the effect is absorbing.

99. Spring Water

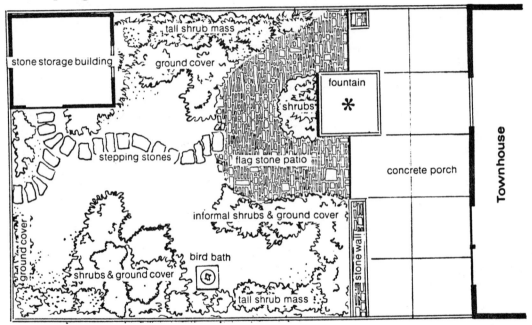

With stone patio, stone paths, lush foliage and a continuous flow of water, capture the feel of a mountain trail. The fountain lends coolness to the garden as well.

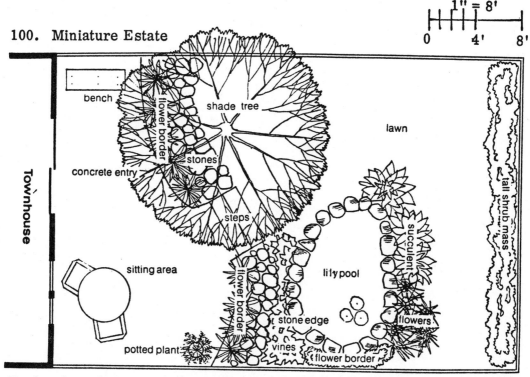

100. Miniature Estate

1" = 8'
0 4' 8'

bench

shade tree

flower border

stones

concrete entry

steps

lawn

Townhouse

sitting area

flower border

lily pool

succulent

tall shrub mass

stone edge

flowers

potted plant

vines

flower border

Pool and garden wall give added depth to this small garden. Water lilies are a must with this setting and you can find varieties that have magnificent flowers.

119

101. Beauty Is In the Eyes Of the Beholder

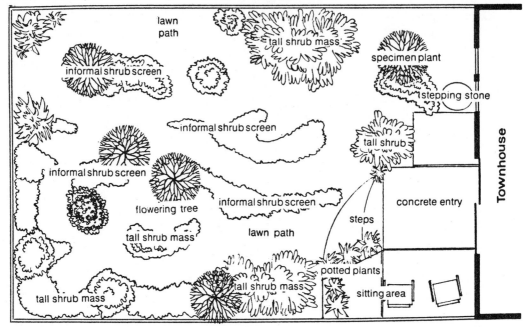

Use shrubs that stimulate your sense of touch, smell, hearing and/or sight.
Attract birds with berry bushes, low trees and/or a bird feeder.
Display your favorite shrubs; organize them into a maze.
Create a personally designed garden.

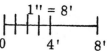

1" = 8'

0   4'   8'

Townhouse

NOTES:

PART III: PLANT SUGGESTIONS—THE BASIC BUILDING BLOCKS

Use these plant suggestions for designing, but don't stop here. There are hundreds of plants that will work for your garden. This list is for ideas. When you visit your local garden center or arboretum, you may decide to choose other plants.

The plants are listed according to the design labels that they most closely match, but they could be used elsewhere. Don't let this list limit your originality.

SHADE TREES (40'-100')

Ash, Green—*Fraxinus pennsylvanica lanceolata*
Beech, American—*Fagus grandiflora*
Beech, European—*Fagus sylvatica*
Ginko—*Ginko biloba*
Gum, Sweet—*Liquidumbar styraciflua*
Japanese Pagoda Tree—*Sophora japonica*
Linden, Little Leaf—*Tilia chordata*
Linden, Pendant Silver—*Tilia petiolaris*
Locust, Honey—*Gleditsia triacanthos*
Maple, Norway—*Acer platanoides*
Maple, Red—*Acer rubrum*
Maple, Sugar—*Acer saccharum*
Oak, Pin—*Quercus palustris*
Oak, Red—*Quercus borealis*
Oak, Willow—*Quercus phellos*

SMALL AND/OR FLOWERING TREES (Up to 40')

Cherry, Autumn Flowering—*Prunus subhirtella*
Cherry, Weeping—*Prunus subhirtella pendula*
Cherry, Yoshino—*Prunus yedoensis*
Crabapple—*Malus*—many species & varieties
Dogwood, Flowering—*Cornus florida*
Dogwood, Japanese—*Cornus kousa*
Hawthorn, Washington—*Crataegus phaenopyrum*
Lilac, Japanese Tree—*Syringa reticulata*
Magnolia, Saucer—*Magnolia x soulangiana*
Magnolia, Star—*Magnolia stellata*
Maple, Japanese—*Acer palmatum*
Red Bud, Eastern—*Cercis canadensis*
Snow Bell, Japanese—*Styrax japonicus*
Sourwood—*Oxydendron arborum*

EVERGREEN TREES (15' & up)

Cedar, Blue Atlas—*Cedrus atlantica* 'Glauca'
Cedar, Deodara—Cedrus deodara
Fir, Douglas—*Pseudotsuga menziesii*
Fir, White—*Abies concolor*
Hemlock, Canadian—*Tsuga canadensis*
Holly, American—*Ilex opaca*
Magnolia, Southern—*Magnolia grandiflora*
Pine—*Pinus*—many species & varieties
Spruce, Blue—*Picea pungens* 'Glauca'
Spruce, Oriental—*Picea orientalis*
Spruce, Serbian—*Picea omorika*

TALL SHRUB SCREEN OR MASS (5'-15')

Evergreen
Arborvitae, American—*Thuja occidentalis*
Arborvitae, Oriental—*Platycladus orientalis*
Hemlock, Canadian—*Tsuga canadensis*
Holly, Buford—*Ilex cornuta* 'Burfordii'
Holly, Japanese—*Ilex crenata*
Holly, Perney—*Ilex pernyi*
Juniper, Chinese—*Juniperus chinensis*
Viburnum, Leather Leaf—*Viburnum rhytidophyllum*

Yew, Anglojap—*Taxus x media*
Yew, Japanese—*Taxus cuspidata*
Yew, Japanese Plum—*Cephelotaxus harringtonia*

Deciduous
Bayberry, Southern—*Myrica cerifera*
Cotoneaster, Spreading—*Cotoneaster divaricata*
Euonymus, Winged—*Euonymus alatus*
Honeysuckle, Tatarian—*Lonicera tatarica*
Honeysuckle, Winter—*Lonicera fragrantissima*
Privet, Amur—*Ligustrum amurense*
Quince, Flowering—*Chaenomeles speciosa*
Viburnum, Burkwood—*Viburnum x burkwoodii*

FLOWERING SHRUBS (3'-10')

Evergreen
Andromeda, Japanese—*Pieris japonica*
Camellia, Japanese—*Camellia japonica*
Camellia, Sasanqua—*Camellia sasanqua*
Cherry Laurel—*Prunus laurocerasus*
Laurel, Mountain—*Kalmia latifolia*
Oregon Grape Holly—*Mahonia aquafolium*
Rhododendron & Azalea—many species & varieties

FLOWERING SHRUBS

Deciduous
Cinquefoil, Bush—*Potentilla fruticosa*
Forsythia, Showey Border—*Forsythia x intermedia*
Lilac, Chinese—*Syringa chinensis*
Spice Bush—*Lindera benzoin*
Sweetshrub, Common—*Calycanthus floridus*
Rhododendron and Azalea—many species & varieties
Viburnum, Koreanspire—*Viburnum cariesii*
Witchhazel, Chinese—*Hamamelis mollis*

LOW SHRUBS (1'-5')

Evergreen
Dwarf Conifers—many species and varieties
Juniper, Andorra—*Juniperus horizontalis*
Holly, Chinese—*Ilex cornuta* 'Rotunda'
Leucothoe, Drooping—*Leucothoe fontanesiana*
Skimmia—*Skimmia japonica*
Yew, English—*Taxus baccata* 'Repandens'

Deciduous
Cotoneaster, Rockspray—*Cotoneaster horizontalis*
Jasmine, Winter—*Jasminum nudiflorum*

Quince, Japanese—*Chaenomeles japonica*
Spirea, Bumald—*Spirea x bumalda*
Viburnum, Cranberry—*Viburnum opulus* 'Nanum'

GROUND COVER

Evergreen
Bearberry—*Arctostaphylos uva-ursi*
Heath—*Erica carnea*
Heather—*Caluna vulgaris*
Ivy, English—*Hedera helix*
Japanese Spurge—*Pachisandra terminalis*
Pachistima—*Pachistima canbyi*
Periwinkle—*Vinca minor*
Sweet Box—*Sarcococca hookerana humilis*
Winter Creeper—*Euonymus fortunei*

Deciduous & Perennial
Cotoneaster, Weeping Willow—*Cotoneaster salicifolia* 'Repens'
Daylily—*Hemerocallis* (many species)
Lily-of-the-Valley—*Convalleria majalis*
Lily Turf—*Liriope spicata*
Plantain Lilies—*Hosta lancifolia* and *undulato*
Stonecrop—*Sedum* (many species)

VINES

Bittersweet—*Celastrus articulatus* 'Thunb'
Clematis (many species)
Honeysuckle, Halls—*Lonicera japonica* 'Haliana'
Trumpet Vine—*Campsis radicans*

FLOWERS

There are hundreds of annuals and perennials to choose from at your local garden centers.

FOLIAGE PLANTS

Choose these plants for interest of leaf color or leaf texture.

SPECIMEN PLANT

A plant that appeals to you for its special characteristics, such as growth habit, and one that can stand alone in the landscape.

SUCCULENTS

Planting spaces for succulents can also serve as fair-weather display areas for your interior plants.

Joel M. Lerner is in the business of creating, developing, designing, licensing and marketing original design concepts. He is a consultant on design development to corporations and individuals, by appointment only.

An 8" x 12" enlargement of your design from this book, labeled with recommended plants, is available from Joel M. Lerner Environmental Design, P.O. Box 15121, Chevy Chase, Maryland 20815. Cables: LERNSCAPE.